KELTIC CREATURES FOR KIDS 3

Kathy O'Meara

Perelandra
Design

This small (5x8) book contains 19 drawings of Keltic Creatures inspired by the Book of Kells. These whimisical characters are geared to appeal to younger children.

Books by Kathy O'Meara

Keltic Crosses Coloring
Keltic Crosses Coloring 2
Keltic Alphabet Coloring: Capital Letters
Keltic Alphabet Coloring: Lower Case Letters
Keltic Coloring: Knots & Numbers
Keltic Coloring: Knotted Nature
Keltic Alphabet Coloring 2: Capital Letters
Keltic Alphabet Coloring 2: Lower Case Letters
Keltic Creatures Coloring
Keltic Creatures For Kids
Keltic Creatures For Kids 2
Keltic Creatures For Kids 3
Keltic Knots For Kids

Stained Glass "Window" Patterns

Spring Flowers
Summer Flowers
Autumn
Circle of Life
Keltic Christian

International Standard Book Number

ISBN-13: 978-1727588873
ISBN-10: 1727588878

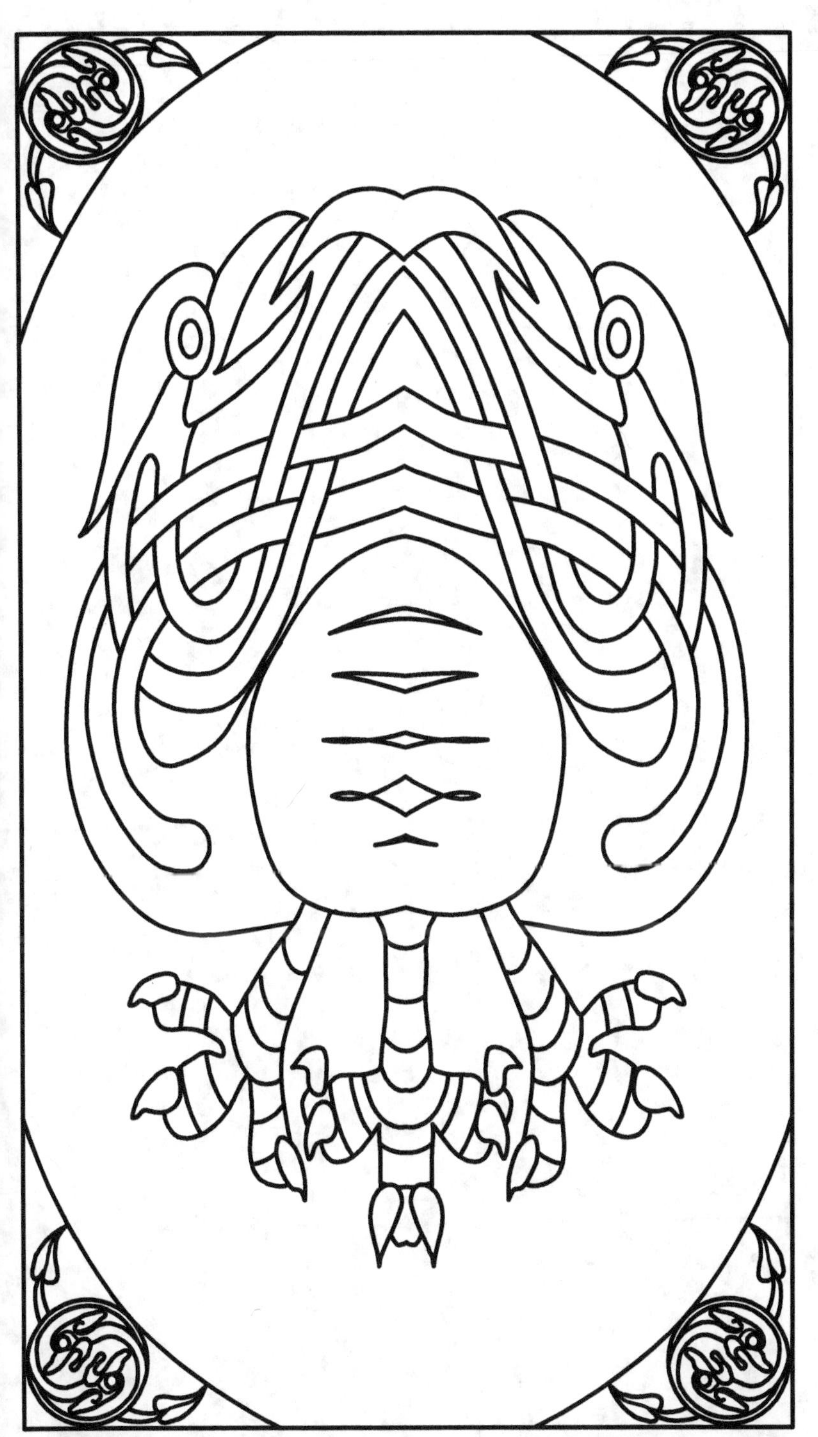

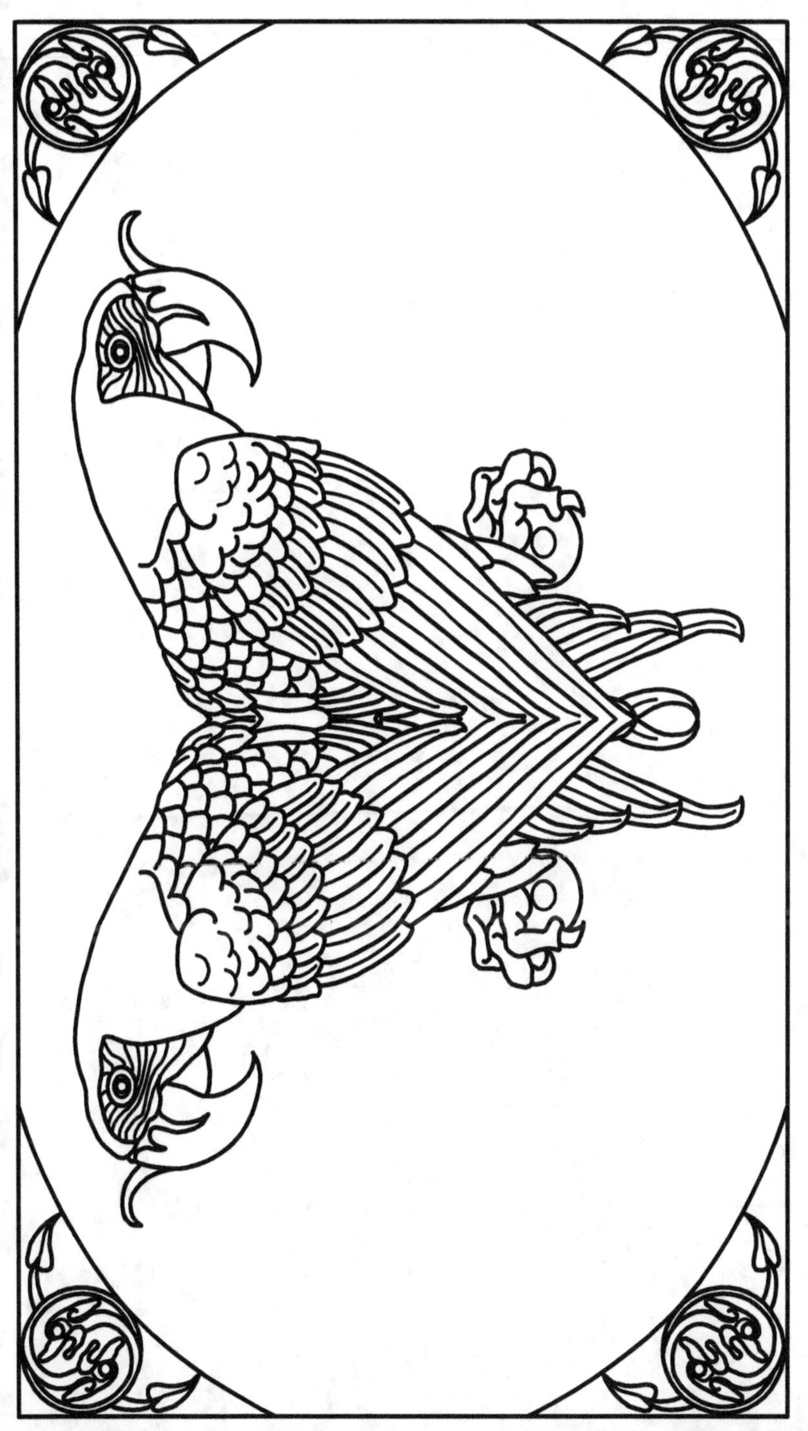

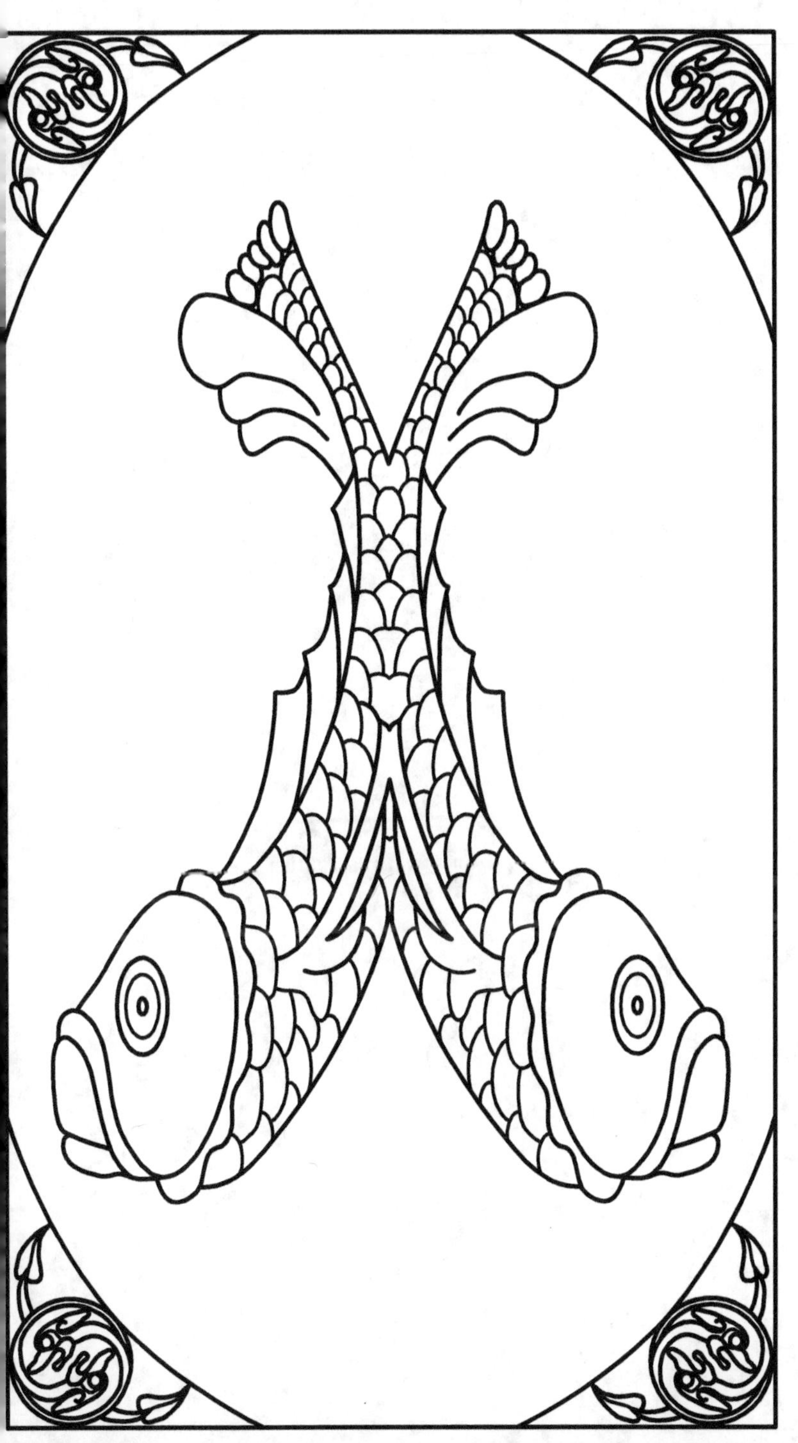